Contents

Aerial view of a ringfort at Lisnabin, Co. Westmeath. On the right in the next field a ringbarrow, crowned with a bush, can be seen beside a pond, (photo - L. Swan). The cover illustration is based on this photograph.

DUBLIN
PUBLISHED BY THE
STATIONERY OFFICE

To be purchased through any Bookseller, or directly from the
GOVERNMENT PUBLICATIONS OFFICE, SUN ALLIANCE HOUSE, MOLESWORTH STREET, DUBLIN 2.

Text by C. Manning.

Design and cover illustration by Aislinn Adams. Other illustrations by P. Coffey.
ISBN 0 7076 0035 9
3rd Edition 1991.

Introduction

By any standard the Irish countryside is very rich in physical remains of the past in the form of archaeological sites and monuments. This remarkable heritage and resource has, however, come under increasing threat in the past couple of decades and as a result many fine monuments, containing much valuable information about the past, have been destroyed or badly damaged.

An archaeological survey of the country is in progress and Sites and Monuments Records have been produced on a county basis. These consist of lists of known archaeological sites accompanied by copies of the 6″ maps with the sites marked on them. The ultimate aim is to produce a detailed published survey on every county but this will take many years. In the meantime archaeological inventories have been published for a number of counties as well as the detailed survey for Co. Louth. The omission of a site from the maps or from any of these surveys does not mean that it is not important as many sites have yet to be discovered.

This booklet has been written for the layman, particularly in the hope that it will assist farmers and others involved in developments, that cause ground disturbance, to identify ancient monuments and thereby secure their preservation. It is also aimed at young people to make them aware of the rich heritage of monuments in Ireland and of the need to safeguard it for future generations. Emphasis is placed on the monument types most frequently encountered or most likely to go unrecognised rather than on the more impressive and well-known monuments many of which are already protected. For information on these better known sites and for general information on the archaeology of Ireland the reader is referred to the books listed on page 24.

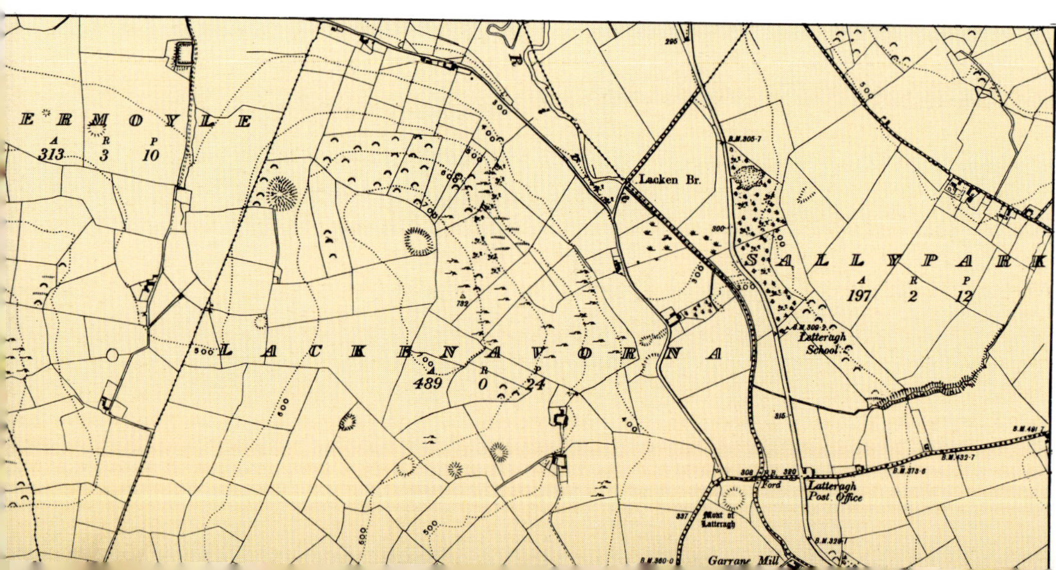

A section of an Ordnance Survey 6 inch map showing ringforts, a rectangular moated site and a motte. (Co. Tipperary; sheet 27. By permission of the Government, Permit No. 4472).

Ringforts

These are undoubtedly the commonest monuments on the landscape and the ones most often under threat. They are found in every county and are known by various names (fort, rath, *dún, lios* etc.). Basically the ringfort is a space surrounded by an earthen bank formed of material thrown up from a fosse or ditch immediately outside the bank. Generally they vary from 25-50 metres in diameter, are usually circular but can also be oval or D-shaped. Some have more than one bank and ditch but such examples are rarer than the simple type. In some areas, especially in the west of Ireland, a massive stone wall enclosed the site in place of a bank and ditch. This type of ringfort is called a caher, cashel or stone fort and well preserved examples may have terraces and steps in the inner face of the wall. Most of these stone forts have been heavily robbed of stone to build roads or field fences and often only traces of the wall survive.

Both types of ringfort were erected as protected enclosures around farmsteads mainly during the Early Christian period (*c.* 500 – 1100 AD). The dwelling houses and other buildings were generally dry-stone or timber built and the remains of stone structures are sometimes visible. It

A cashel or stone fort at Leacanabuaile, Co. Kerry, after excavation and conservation. The conserved lower portions of dry-stone buildings can be seen within the fort. (photo – C. Brogan).

Diagram of a souterrain or underground passage. a, Entrance. b, Passage. c, Corbelled Chamber. These are sometimes found during ploughing, quarrying or house building.

Souterrains

A feature often found in ringforts is an underground passage or souterrain (popularly known as a cave or tunnel). They are usually built of stone but can also be tunnelled into rock or compact clay or gravel. Souterrains are sometimes found apparently independent of any enclosure and are also found in Early Christian ecclesiastical enclosures. They were used as places of refuge and possibly also for storage and can be encountered unexpectedly during ploughing, bulldozing or quarrying. These structures can be unsafe, especially if recently uncovered and should be treated with extreme caution.

Tree covered crannóg in Kilcorran Lough, Co. Monaghan. (photo – C. Brogan).

A ringfort in hilly terrain with remains of an internal rectangular hut at Ballymakellett, Co. Louth. (photo – C. Brogan).

Interior view of a souterrain looking from the chamber out along the passage at Benagh, Co. Louth. (photo – C. Brogan).

is only during archaeological excavation that the traces of wooden structures can be found. Sometimes, especially in permanent pasture land or rocky terrain, ancient field systems, associated with ringforts, survive.

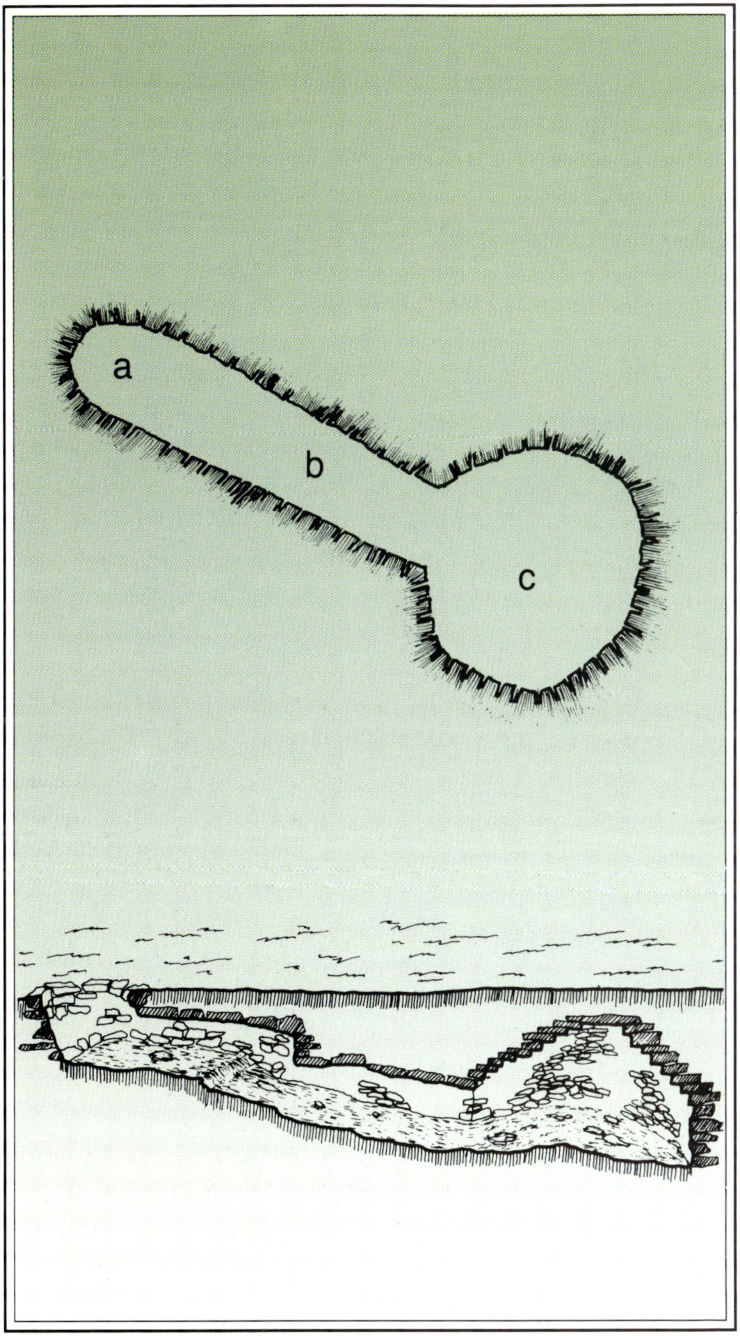

Crannógs

These are small circular man-made islands in lakes or marshland serving the same function as ringforts and used during much the same period. Crannógs were made up of layers of material such as lake-mud, brushwood and stones with a palisade of closely-set wooden stakes around the perimeter to consolidate the structure and act as a defensive barrier. The stumps of these stakes are often visible, preserved by the water logged conditions, which also preserve other wooden and leather objects making these sites particularly interesting to archaeologists. Drainage schemes often leave crannógs high and dry on the foreshore in which situation they can be difficult to recognise.

Hillforts & Promontory forts

Some early forts were built making maximum use of naturally defended positions such as low hills and promontories. Hillforts are large enclosures delimited by a bank and ditch or a stone wall enclosing the top of a hill. In some cases there are a number of lines of defence widely separated from each other. These must have been tribal rather than family units and were used mainly during the Iron Age (c. 300 BC – 500 AD).

Many suitable cliff headlands around the coast and some inland were defended by the erection of earthen ramparts or massive stone walls cutting off the neck of the promontory. These promontory forts. which vary greatly in size, usually have the element *dún* in their names and are generally assigned to the Iron Age.

The promontory fort called Dún Dúchathair on high cliffs on Inishmore, Aran Islands, Co. Galway. A massive dry-stone wall with an entrance at one end defends the interior where the remains of a few structures survive close to the wall. (photo – C. Brogan).

An aerial view of the massive hillfort at Mooghaun, Co. Clare. Three large concentric walls enclose this hilltop and there are also two smaller enclosures of ringfort size which appear to be later in date. (photo – L. Swan).

Early ecclesiastical enclosures

A large proportion of the old church sites and graveyards around the country are on the sites of Early Christian ecclesiastical foundations which were originally surrounded by large enclosures, often circular or oval in plan, and usually far more extensive than the surviving graveyards. In some instances the entire enclosing bank, ditch or stone wall survives but more often the line of the enclosure is only indicated by curving field boundaries or cropmarks or low earthworks visible only from the air. As well as an early church and burial ground these enclosures contained the dwellings and workshops of a community sometimes approaching the size of a town. As the buildings were generally of

Early ecclesiastical enclosure at Moyne, near Shrule, Co. Mayo. An ancient wall here encloses an area much larger than the present graveyard. Note the earthworks forming further divisions within the enclosure. (Photo – L. Swan).

The early monastic site of Lusk, Co. Dublin. Some of the roads of the present-day village follow the curve of the early enclosure. Centrally placed in the graveyard is a 19th-century church attached to a medieval tower which incorporates an early round tower. (photo - L. Swan).

wood nothing survives in the enclosures above the ground while in the graveyards there is often a ruined medieval parish church. These enclosures vary in diameter from *c.* 30m to as large as *c.* 400m.

In some cases there is no surviving graveyard or merely an old graveyard without any inscribed headstones. Such sites were often used for the burial of unbaptised children during the last few centuries and are known by various names (killeen, *ceallúnach* etc.). *Bullauns* (boulders with round basin-shaped hollows in them) are often found on early church sites while *Holy Wells* may be situated close to them. Professional archaeological advice should be sought before considering any works or development within 100 metres of an old graveyard.

Linear earthworks & roadways

Large banks with an accompanying ditch or ditches running for great distances across the countryside probably acted as territorial boundaries and impediments to the driving off of cattle. Such linear earthworks are generally only well preserved for short stretches and the best known example is the Black Pig's Dyke, parts of which survive in counties Monaghan, Cavan and Leitrim. Other linear earthworks are the Worm Ditch, the Dane's Cast and the *Claidhe Dubh.*

Ancient roadways can also be found running for long distances but, because they have for the most part been obliterated by modern roads or cultivation, they are often now only in evidence across mountain terrain or across bogs where they are known as toghers. Many toghers were built of timber planks laid lengthways on crossbeams and kept in place by pegs driven into the bog. Well preserved examples have been found during turfcutting.

Togher or timber roadway across a bog at Corlea, Co. Longford as uncovered by archaeological excavation. This togher was built in 148 B.C. during the Iron Age. (photo – B. Raftery).

Fulachta Fiadh & Horizontal mills

Ancient cooking places called *Fulachta Fiadh* are one of the least well-known monument types, often not recognised as ancient features and seldom marked on the maps. They usually survive as small horseshoe-shaped mounds made up mainly of small pieces of blackened stone and situated close to a water source or in marshy or formerly marshy ground. A rectangular pit, lined with wooden planks or stone slabs to form a trough, is invariably found during archaeological excavation under the open part of the horseshoe-shaped mound. Water was heated in the trough by rolling hot stones into it from a fire close by. It has been proved by experiment that water can be boiled in this way and meat cooked in it. The hot stones often shattered on contact with the water and the mound was formed as a result of shovelling the broken stones out of the trough so that it could be used

Fulacht Fiadh at Rathlogan, Co. Kilkenny. It has the normal horseshoe-shaped mound and its location in marshy ground close to a stream is typical. (photo - T. Condit).

again. The timber trough or part of it often survives in the damp conditions usually prevailing on these sites.

The practice of using these sites persisted from at least the Bronze Age down to the historic period and the method of using them is described in early texts. They can occur in groups and are frequently encountered during land reclamation and field drainage.

Another monument type found in similar situations is the horizontal mill. These are of rare occurrence and portions of wooden structures, displaying sophisticated carpentry techniques, have been revealed during excavation. These mill sites have been dated to the Early Christian period but are generally not recognisable on the surface.

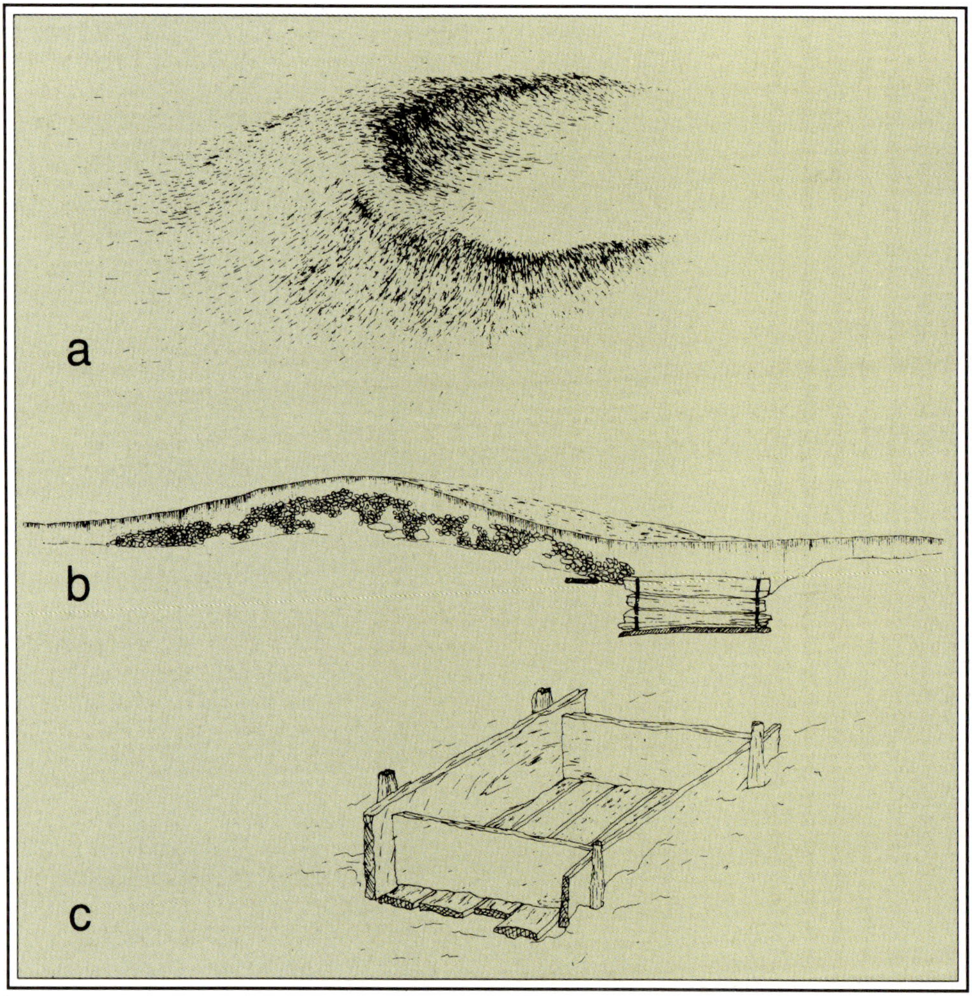

Diagram of a Fulacht Fiadh.
a, Crescent - shaped mound
b, Section through wooden trough and mound
c, View of trough.

Aerial view of Deer Park or Magheraghanrush Court-tomb, Co. Sligo. This fine example has a central elongated court with burial chambers opening off each end. Most of the cairn has been robbed over the centuries leaving only the large structural stones. (photo – C. Brogan).

Megalithic tombs

As the word 'megalithic' signifies, these
structures were built of large stones.
Basically they consist of a burial chamber
or chambers, built of large uprights and
roofed over in stone, originally contained
within a cairn (heap of stones) or a clay
mound but accessible through an
entrance. In most cases the cairns have
been largely robbed of stone leaving
only the ruined chamber popularly
referred to as a dolmen, giant's grave,
druid's altar or Diarmuid and Gráinne's
Bed. Many are given these or similar
names on the 6 inch O.S. map while
others are not marked at all. Megalithic
tombs can be divided into four main
classes: Court-tombs, Portal-tombs,
Passage-tombs and Wedge-tombs.

Court-tombs are found mainly in the
northern half of the country and are so
called because they generally have a
curved forecourt at the entrance to the
tomb at one end of a long straight-sided
cairn. As with all megalithic tombs the
cairn may be partially or totally robbed
and often only the upright stones of the
chamber survive.

Portal-tombs are found mainly in the
northern part of the country and in South
Leinster and Waterford. Some of the well
preserved examples are among the most
impressive megalithic tombs in the
country. Their name is derived from the

two large upright stones forming the entrance or portal of the chamber. The often massive capstone is supported on these and on the lower back and side stones. It is seldom that any remains of a cairn survive.

Passage-tombs are found mainly in concentrations, known as cemeteries, of which that in the bend of the Boyne around Newgrange is the most famous. In plan they consist essentially of a round mound or cairn with a passage leading from the edge to a chamber within. Many of them are sited on hilltops and in some cases the structural stones of the tomb are decorated. These along with the Portal and Court-tombs belong to the Neolithic or New Stone Age period (*c.* 4000 – 2000 BC).

The fourth tomb type, the Wedge-tomb, has been assigned to the succeeding Early Bronze Age (after 2000 BC). This type is more widespread than the others with many occurring in Munster where other tomb types are very rare. These tombs originally consisted of a rectangular chamber often narrowing and declining in height towards the back (hence the name) and roofed with slabs. The cairn can be round, oval or D-shaped.

Portal-tomb at Kilclooney More, Co. Donegal. This photograph shows the matched pair of tall portal stones at the entrance and the large and impressive capstone. (photo – C. Brogan).

Wedge-tomb at Caheraphuca, Co. Clare. As their name implies these tombs are often wedge shaped both in plan and section. (photo – C. Brogan).

Passage-tomb cairns on a mountain at Carrowkeel, Co. Sligo. These are part of a cemetery or group of passage-tombs at Carrowkeel. (photo – C. Brogan).

Mounds, Cairns & Barrows

Circular mounds or cairns of rounded profile and varying greatly in size are known in most parts of the country. These are generally burial mounds but may cover any one of a number of different types of burial (Passage-tombs, or other Neolithic or Early Bronze Age burials). It is sometimes possible to classify robbed or denuded examples if part of the structure is exposed.

The practice of burying in cists, box-like structures made of stone slabs, is first found in the Neolithic period. These large cists containing one or two burials accompanied by decorated Neolithic pottery are found covered by round mounds and to date occur only in the southern part of the country.

Early Bronze Age cists are found also under round mounds but are mostly smaller than the Neolithic ones and a number of them are usually found in the

one mound. The burials in them can be
either cremated or unburnt and decorated
pottery, either food vessels or urns, is
generally found with them. Similar burials
are also found without the protection of a
cist but accompanied by the pottery. Early
Bronze Age burials can also occur
individually or in flat cemeteries where
there is no mound. Such burials are often
found unexpectedly during sand and
gravel quarrying.

Often difficult to see on the ground are
small mounds with encircling ditch and
bank known as ringbarrows. These can
vary in size from about 4 metres across to
as much as 20 metres. Usually the bank is
outside the ditch and sometimes there is
little or no mound within. They can occur
in clusters and are often not marked on
the 6 inch map. Excavation has shown
that they are burial monuments usually
containing cremations of Bronze or Iron
Age date.

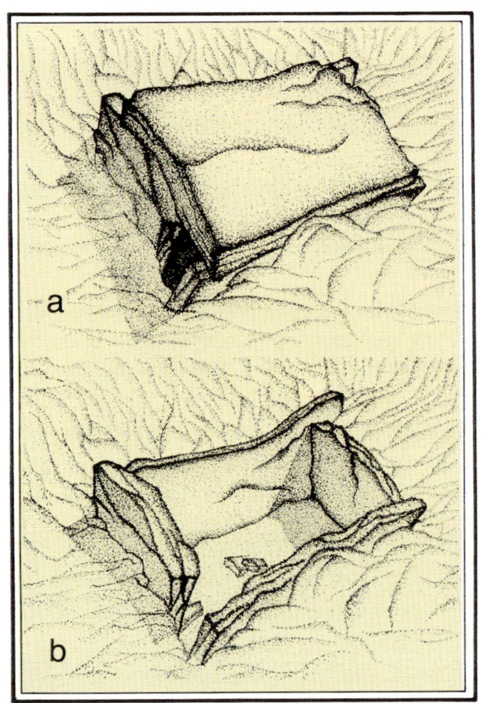

↑

Isolated cist graves are generally
found by accident when a plough
or bulldozer removes the
capstone. They contain burials
which are usually cremated, and
often a pottery vessel. Diagram of
a cist grave: a. with capstone; b.
without capstone.

A ringbarrow at Rathnarrow, Co.
Westmeath with archaeological
excavation in progress around it.
(photo – C. Brogan).

Stone circles, Alignments, Standing stones & Rock art

The stone circles which are found in certain parts of the country such as the West Cork/South Kerry area were apparently used for ritual purposes. Some circles have a dozen or more upright stones while the smallest ones have only five stones and measure 2 to 4 metres across.

Alignments or straight lines of three or more closely set standing stones are known especially in areas where stone circles occur. Both types date from the Bronze Age.

Single standing stones known by various names (*gallán, dallán, líagán,* long stone etc.) are of more widespread occurrence but are not necessarily all of one period or one purpose. Some have been shown to mark prehistoric burials while others may have served some other commemorative or ritual function. They vary in height considerably, up to a maximum of about 5 metres. Some smaller upright stones can have crosses inscribed on them from Early Christian times or Ogham inscriptions. The latter is an ancient alphabet consisting of dots and strokes cut along the edge or edges of a stone. The bulk of these ogham stones are found in Counties Cork, Kerry and Waterford.

Ogham inscribed standing stone on Dunmore Head, at the westernmost tip of the Dingle Peninsula, Co. Kerry. (photo - F. Moore).

Stone circle at Bohonagh, Co. Cork. (photo - C. Brogan).

They are often found lying flat or reused as lintels in souterrains or other later structures.

Rock outcrops and natural boulders were sometimes inscribed with cup and circles, concentric circles and other designs during the Bronze Age.

Medieval earthworks

The most impressive of these is the motte, popularly called a moat, which can survive as a very large steep-sided mound of earth with a flat top. These were constructed during the early phases of the Anglo-Norman settlement in the 12th and 13th centuries. Originally there would have been a wooden tower and palisade on top and many examples have an attached enclosure called a bailey which would have contained houses and other buildings. During an attack the motte itself would have served as the main strong point and last resort.

In certain areas Anglo-Norman settlers constructed square or rectangular enclosures called moated sites. Their

Rock art on outcropping rock at Kealduff Upper, Co. Kerry. (photo – C. Manning).

Motte at Clonard, Co. Meath. (photo – C. Brogan).

main defensive feature was a wide (often waterfilled) fosse with an internal bank and sometimes a slight external bank. As with ringforts, which they resemble in scale, these enclosures protected a house and outbuildings usually built of wood.

The Anglo-Normans also founded towns and villages in the areas they settled and while some of these are still important centres others have dwindled in size or become deserted. These deserted settlements can cover large areas of ground and where grazing only has taken place they can survive as complex systems of small banks which can sometimes be rationalised as the remains of houses, outbuildings and property boundaries arranged around a street or streets. Often there is an old church and graveyard nearby and a castle, motte or tower house.

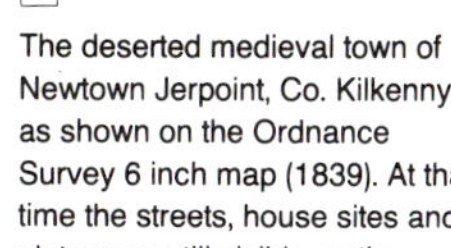
➡

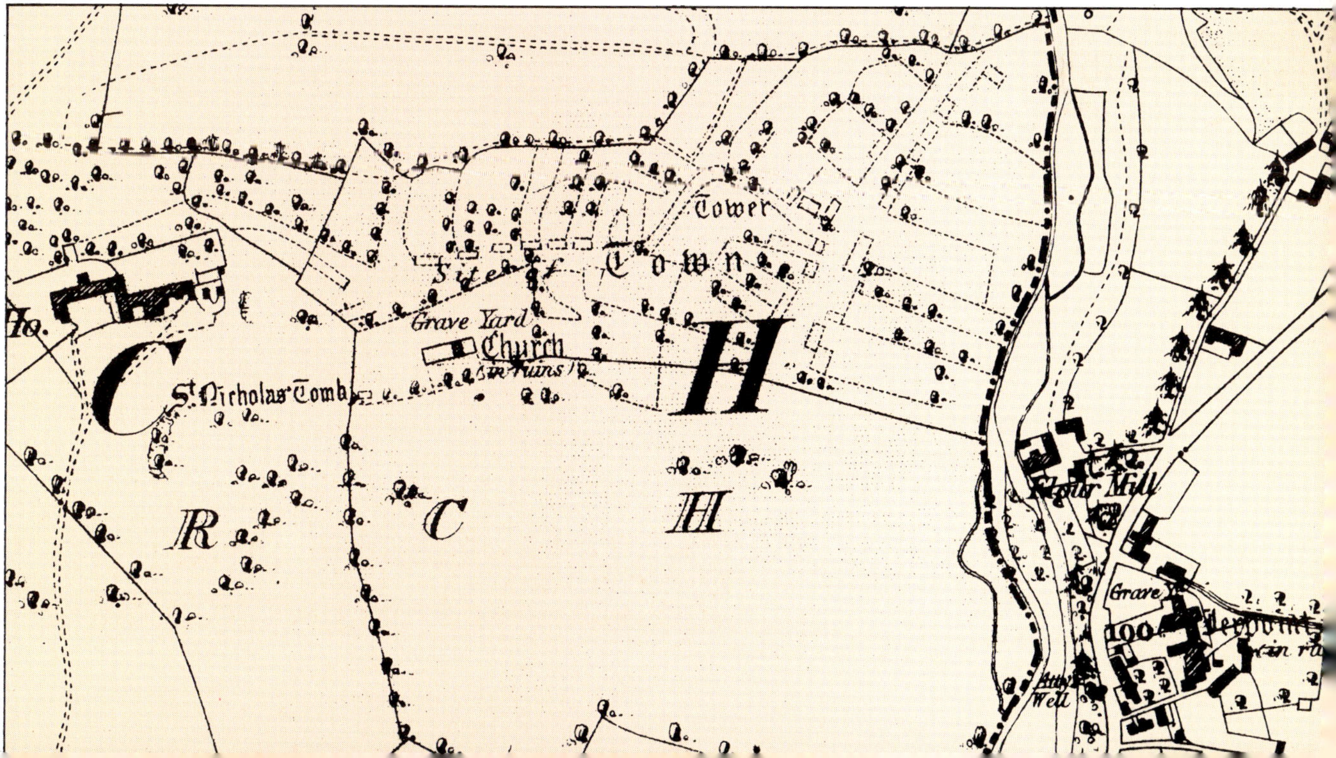

Moated site at Grove, Co. Kilkenny. The fosse or moat still fills with water during wet weather. This site is not marked on any edition of the Ordnance Survey map. (photo - T. Barry).

⬇

The deserted medieval town of Newtown Jerpoint, Co. Kilkenny as shown on the Ordnance Survey 6 inch map (1839). At that time the streets, house sites and plots were still visible on the ground.

Medieval buildings

Medieval castles come in a great variety of shapes and sizes and are usually marked on the 6 inch O.S. maps. Also marked as castles on the maps are the tall structures of the later Medieval period (15th-16th centuries) which are more correctly referred to as tower houses. Many of these are remarkably well preserved.

Medieval churches and monasteries are often surrounded by graveyards under the care of local authorities but some are unprotected in open fields. Again these are normally marked on the maps or are known of locally.

Some castles and churches have been largely removed over the years and no visible trace or just a few humps in the ground may survive. Such sites of churches or castles (frequently marked as such on the maps) are of archaeological importance and can yield much information if properly excavated. Earthworks of a settlement or enclosure are often found surrounding or close to castles, tower houses and churches and even if these are not in evidence the area surrounding any of these structures should not be disturbed. Professional archaeological advice should be sought in defining this area.

Aerial view of a tower house at Rockstown, Co. Limerick. Traces of a pear-shaped enclosure or bawn can be seen enclosing the top of the rocky knoll on which the tower house was built. (photo - C. Brogan).

Miscellaneous monuments

There are many other ancient monuments in our countryside which are worth preserving. Among these are fortified houses of the 16th and 17th centuries, star-shaped artillery forts of the same period, Martello towers, old houses and mansions of architectural interest and landlord's follies. Of a less imposing nature are isolated house and hut sites including booley huts in mountain areas and the stone-corbelled huts common in Kerry called *clocháns*. There are also many interesting structures such as old bridges, sweat houses, lime and corn-drying kilns, ice houses, pigeon houses and old light houses. A specialist study in itself is industrial archaeology which is concerned with industrial monuments such as windmills and watermills of all sorts, old factories, canals, mines, etc.

Aerial view of Creevelea Franciscan Friary near Dromahair, Co. Leitrim. The long church has a central tower while the domestic buildings were built around an open square cloister garth. (photo - C. Brogan).

A recently restored 19th-century mill with its mill wheel on the banks of the Funcheon at Glanworth, Co. Cork. On the cliff behind is Glanworth Castle dating from the 13th to 17th centuries. (photo - C. Brogan).

Sites not showing on the surface

Very few prehistoric habitation sites have been found in comparison with the number of known burial and ritual monuments. This is due to the fact that the houses were generally flimsy structures made of wood or other perishable materials and not normally defended by large walls or banks. Such habitation sites are usually found only by accident during the excavation of some other monument or as a result of the finding of small artifacts during ploughing or other land disturbance. Any works that involve considerable disturbance of the ground surface such as drainage and land improvement works, quarrying, road and building construction and pipe laying can uncover hitherto unknown sites of all types including monuments that had been totally levelled prior to the first edition of the Ordnance Survey maps. All such finds should be reported without delay to the Chief Archaeologist (address below).

The site of a circular post-and-wattle house during excavation at Lackenavorna, Co. Tipperary. This photograph illustrates how archaeological features can survive in certain circumstances very close to the surface. (photo – C. Manning).

A complex series of cropmarks showing in a field of corn in the townland of Bracklin, Co. Westmeath. Cropmarks result from buried features (such as ditches or wall foundations) causing differences in crop growth which may be visible from the air. Archaeological sites with no surface features can be detected in this way. (photo – L. Swan).

Another area of work where interesting discoveries can be made is in the cutting of turf both in the raised bogs common in the Midlands and the blanket bogs covering much upland terrain especially in the West. Toghers (wooden trackways across bogs) are the main monument type found in raised bogs but blanket bog can cover many types of monuments including megalithic tombs, cairns, stone circles, house sites and field walls. A massive Neolithic field system associated with a court-tomb and habitation sites was discovered in North Mayo during turf cutting.

Archaeological excavation

Modern archaeological excavation is a highly skilled activity requiring much expertise in the recovery of the evidence and in its interpretation and publication. Contrary to popular opinion archaeologists do not excavate in order to find gold or other valuable objects. Rather, their intention is to get the maximum information about the past from the ground. Objects found in an excavation are important principally because of their recorded association with other objects, structures, layers or features. For this reason it is important that unqualified persons should not undertake archaeological excavation and if by accident a discovery is made everything should be left as it is without any further uncovering of the object or feature or any other disturbance of the immediate area until an official inspection has been made.

Section 26(1) of the National Monuments Act 1930 makes it unlawful to excavate for archaeological purposes without a licence from the Commissioners of Public Works. Their consent is also required to use a metal detector for the purpose of searching for archaeological objects according to section 2 of the National Monuments (Amendment) Act 1987. Such consents are normally issued only to qualified and experienced archaeologists.

Relevant authorities

Queries regarding ancient sites or monuments should be addressed to:

**The Director,
National Monuments and Historic Properties Service,
Office of Public Works,
51 St. Stephen's Green,
Dublin 2.
Telephone (01) 613111**

Reports of monuments in danger or new discoveries should be directed to the

Chief Archaeologist

at the same address.

The discovery of ancient artifacts or archaeological objects should be reported without delay to the Garda Síochána or to:

**The Director,
National Museum of Ireland,
Kildare St.,
Dublin 2.
Telephone (01) 618811.**

(see National Monuments Acts, 1930-1987).

Further reading

S.P. Ó Ríordáin *Antiquities of the Irish Countryside* (5th edition, revised by R. de Valera). Methuen 1979.

P. Harbison *Guide to the National Monuments of Ireland.* Gill and Macmillan 1975.

Historic Monuments of Northern Ireland: An Introduction and Guide. H.M.S.O. Belfast 1983.

E. Evans *Prehistoric and Early Christian Ireland: A Guide.* Batsford 1966.

M. Herity and G. Eogan *Ireland in Prehistory.* Routledge and Kegan Paul 1977.

P. Harbison, *Pre-Christian Ireland.* Thames and Hudson 1988.

M.J. O'Kelly, *Early Ireland.* Cambridge University Press 1989.

T.B. Barry, *The Archaeology of Medieval Ireland.* Methuen 1987.

N. Edwards, *The Archaeology of Early Medieval Ireland.* Batsford 1990.